Alexithymia: What it's like to Feel

Yanise Hoetmer

Presentation by *BookLeaf Publishing*

Web: www.bookleafpub.com

E-mail: info@bookleafpub.com

ISBN: 9789395950114

First edition 2022

DEDICATION

"Dedicated to everyone who wonders if I am writing about them. I am."

ACKNOWLEDGEMENT

I can't believe this is happening. I want to thank BookLeaf Publishing for making my dreams come true, by publishing something of mine. I want to also thank my family for supporting me and pushing me forward. I want to say thank you to my two best friends, Kaitlyn and Jill, for always having my back and having never-ending support for me. Thank you for being with me in rough times and pushing me towards my dreams. You two mean the world to me and I love you both very much.

PREFACE

To those who feel too much and to those who
feel too little. I hope you find some peace and
comfort in whatever you are feeling. You are not
alone. There is always someone out there, who
is ready to help you with their arm stretched out.
All you have to do is reach out and take it.

Disclaimer: Alexithymia is a medical diagnosis,
I know that now. I have not been diagnosed with
it. I found the definition on Pinterest and I knew
I found the word I was looking for, for my book.

You're always mine

From the day that I first held you
I knew that you were mine
God answers prayers and placed you in my life
I will always love you, as if you were my own
Your name is on my heart as if it was set in stone

Tired eyes and a heavy head
My new little baby sleeps in her bed
I smile down at her with love
I chose you baby, you are enough

I cannot wait to watch you grow
Though my heart aches, when I have to let you
go
The years will go by and time will fly
But remember child, you will always be mine

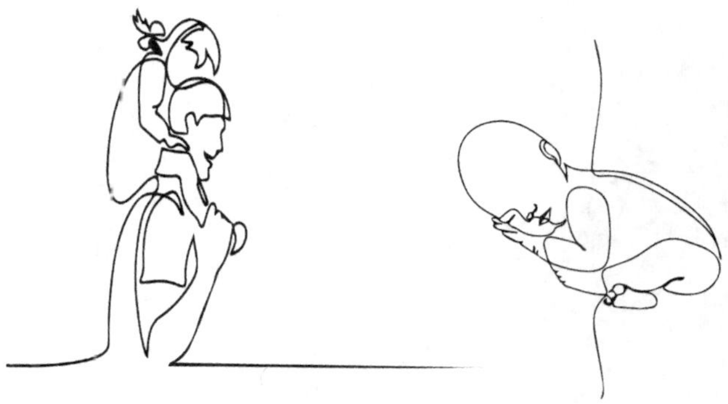

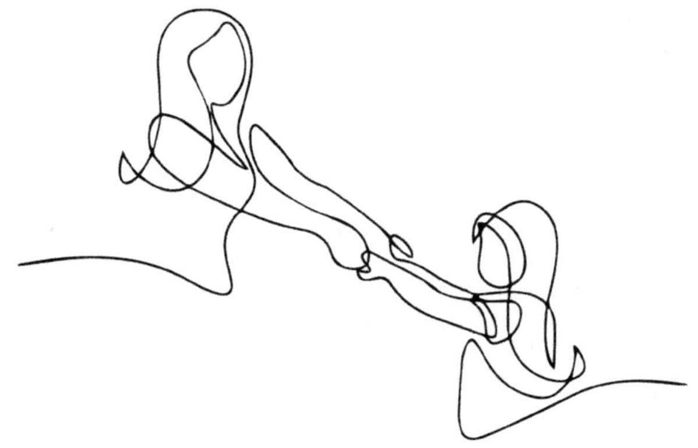

My LORD and My Savior

Oh my LORD, oh my Savior
Let all my praise be yours forever
I will sing of your greatness throughout the earth
You knew I was yours, even before birth
Your never-ending love and saving grace
Keeps me running towards you, to the end of the
race
Your son who died on the cross for me
Is foretold and taught in the prophecies

You will come again on the clouds of Heaven
The earth will shake and quake on trumpet seven
The clouds will roll back and you'll come down
Hear your sons and daughters hallelujahs
resound
The wicked will flee from your sight
The righteous will rejoice at your might
The time has come for us to go Home
The weak and the helpless will never be alone

The LORD has done many mighty things
He sent prophets, priests and kings
One thing we can learn from the past
The LORD's love and mercy is always steadfast
You shall not fear, says the LORD

Do not lose your confidence, for you will have a
rich reward
Keep pushing forward keep running the race
For in the end, you will experience God's saving
grace.

I'm not what you think

Sometimes people are not what you think
Depressed people can smile
And sad people can laugh
Some people are better at putting on a mask
They may seem happy, but really they're not
It sucks pretending, being someone you're not
It's hard to explain how I feel down inside
So I'll put on a smile and put my feelings aside
Don't ask me if I'm okay, because I'll tell a lie
You'll look at me and say, ok, like everythings
fine
My heavy head hurts, everytime I think
All my happiness drains away, like water in a
sink
I want to go to therapy to help clear my mind
But I'm scared to get started, scared to see what
they find
I know I have friends, but it feels like I don't
And when I'm with a group of people, I feel so
alone
Someone please help me, this is my cry for help
I don't know if I can do this, so here's my final
yelp

Love is a Poison

Love is a poison, it affects your thinking
Makes you feel like you're drowning, makes you
feel like you're sinking
Further and farther down in the pit
The pit where everyone seem to be in
I don't want to go, I don't want to join them
Because that means I have to fall in love again
But to fall is to trip, to stumble, to land
To land into something that potentially won't last
But you might say, what about feelings and
intimacy
I say to you, I'd rather drown in the sea
Not that I'm totally against this thing called love
But to get me started, I'd need a push and shove
I'd rather land hard enough to rattle my cage
The cage in which my heart sits, unchanged
The only time I wish something, would take my
breath away
Love is a poison and I've learned this the hard
way
It worms its way into your mind and your brain
It captures your heart and makes you say things
insane
Like, I miss you, and, I love you

These words are just not what I'm looking
forward to
I don't want hear it, I don't want to say it
Because that means I have to let someone in and
commit
Commit to something that won't work out
I don't know why people make such a big deal
about
There's nothing really special about caring about
another
All you get is smooches and being smothered
The holding hands and cutesy smiles
I'd rather be at home crying my eyes out
Love is a poison I now do believe that
But no matter how hard I try, it will always
come back.

A crowded mind

Anxieties and responsibilities are crowded in my head
The depression and sadness keep me heavy in my bed
The weight of the world and everything in it
Keep coming and going, like the tide coming in
I may seem happy, but really I'm not
All this pressure to do something I really don't want
If I don't really love something, then why should I bother
I'd really only being doing it, for the satisfaction of others

Take me Home

Wishing, waiting, wanting
Wishing for time to stop
Waiting for the day to come
Wanting to go to the place called Home
Where every life is destined to go
Where life will continue forever more
When the time will come when people will not
mourn
So everyone come now and prayer
To the heavenly one
Who gives us each a brand new day
In a very special and wonderful way

Darkness please leave

Darkness covers me like a blanket
I can not flee from the feeling
That someone is watching me
Bitter and cold taunt me like a nightmare
Don't they realize that I'm scared?
Pain inside numbs me to the bone
Anxiety, depression free I feel so alone
I used to be so strong now I am weak
I wonder what He thinks of me, maybe a freak
Darkness he wakes me from my sleep
He tell me that I'll never find peace
I beg him to let me go
He shakes his head and says no
I hold myself and start to sob
My mind, my thoughts a thick deep fog
Then I hear a voice in the night
It says come to me, come to light
I look up I shield my eyes
The light is bright I start to cry
There has always been someone who loves me
I never knew, but now I'm free

What it's Like to Drown

My heads just above the water
I don't know what to do
This smile thing is getting hard
I don't know if I'll make it through
Everyone is happy and are on cloud nine
I can't seem to crack a smile without wanting to
cry
Though I know this is only sleepiness
But it never seems to help
Keeping my head above the waves
Is so much work in itself
Now here's a fun fact for you
If you see me laugh or smile
Just know that smile took me awhile
The weight of being tired is dragging me down
Who knows when the time will come
When all I want to do is drown
The waves are surging faster
And all I hear is laughter
No one seems to give a shit
So I sit here at the bottom of the deep dark pit

What Keeps You Up at Night?

Memories, dreams, keep me up late
The good times of long ago
Happy things I can't seem to let go
But I need to
Because it's haunting and filling my mind
I can't seem to distinguish the truth from the lies
They pour in from the left and the right
The hurt and the words cut deeper than a knife
I can't seem to get over the things that I did
I want to go back and take back everything I
said
I roll over once and then again on my back
I stare up at the ceiling, my train of thoughts off
the track
I can't seem to put my running mind at ease
I just can't seem to sleep, someone help me
please
I sit up in bed in and try to forget
But I can't, so I drown in my cold sweat
The bad times come haunt me
The good times are daunting
The monsters in my closet, laugh at my distress
I'd rather deal with them, more or less
So what keeps you up at night?

Is it the monsters or the nightmares?

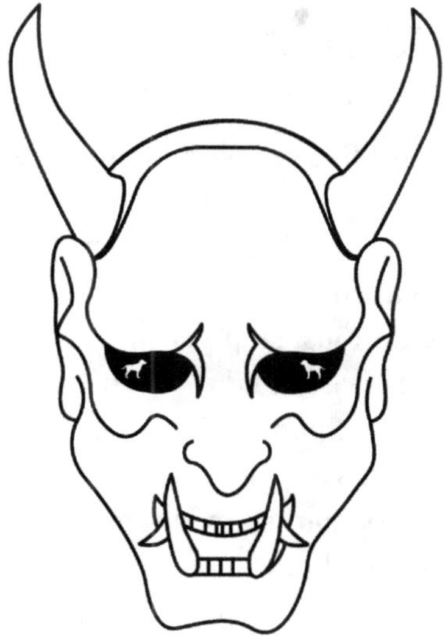

Conversation between the Heart and the Mind

Hey it's late, why are you thinking?- heart
Ya it is, why are you aching? -mind
I'm aching because I can't get over this thing.
This thing called love that I once got. Do I want
it again, or do I just stop?-Heart
I'm thinking I wish I did things better. I want to
go back and do things differently, but I think
right now things are meant to be.
Is that why you hurt so much- mind
Is that why you think so much?- heart
Yes, it is. It's because I want too much- mind
 Yes it is. It's because I care too much-heart
You should stop caring so much-mind
And you should stop wanting- heart
Not needing is like not breathing-mind
Not caring is like not living, I live to care. I just
can't stop. Even if someone doesn't care about
me, I'll never stop- heart
But doesn't that hurt?- mind
Doesn't it hurt you when you think of something
and it happens to be true?- heart
Yes it does, But that doesn't answer my question,
doesn't it hurt to care?- mind
Yes it does hurt. It hurts because I know what it's
like not to be cared for. It hurts because I know

what it feels like to want something and not being able to have it. Answer me this, does it hurt to think of a scenario that will never happen?- heart
Yes it does. It kills to know that my imagination is dangerous. Dangerous for me and dangerous for you. I apologize if I've hurt you in more ways than one, I didn't mean to think of something we both want. -mind
I know that you're sorry, and so am I. I don't mean to carry all these burdens of loving. I wish that I could stop, stop caring for once, but that means stopping you, and I love you too much. -Heart
I love you too, Heart. You make me feel whole, even though sometimes what you feel is too much out of your control. -mind
I'm sorry if sometimes I get carried away, I think I want love, but I'm scared it won't stay.- Heart
I know the feeling because I think too much. I think that maybe one day I'll be enough. But this constant overthinking has gotten me nowhere and I know that maybe one day I won't even get there. -Mind
I hate that I ache, everytime I think of something I've said or done, I want to go back and take back every wrong.-Heart
You know you can't change the past. Even if what you had before didn't last. Please don't

blame yourself, it only makes things harder in the future. -Mind

I don't see much in the future. I'm scared to move forward, to move on. I don't think I can love myself again. I hate the way I ended things.-Heart

Heart, you can't live like this. You need to forgive yourself. -Mind

One day I will Head, one day I can. But at the moment I don't want to love again. -Heart

I feel you heart, I really do. Because right now I don't want to think of the possibilities. -Mind

 For now, Head, let's make a promise to each other, that one day we will heal and to grow, to love and to hope- Heart

To heal, we need to grow, to grow we need to love and to love we need to hope. -Mind

I love you, Head always will, even if you reel and spin. You're amazing in every way, I wouldn't change a thing.- Heart

I love you too, you lump of muscle, you keep me alive and for that I am grateful.-Mind

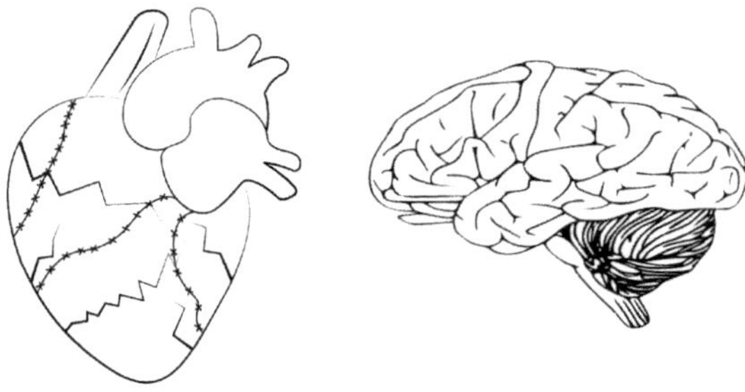

Why is there an "If" in Life?

Why is there an "if" in life?
There is an if in everything
Oh, if only this, if only that
If only I could have that job
If only I didn't feel so miserable
If only I could buy that car
If only he didn't live so far
If only I could have that game
If only things could have stayed the same
The many ifs we have in life
Don't bring us joy, only strife
If only we could've had the talk
If only I could be someone I'm not
If only I could stop pretending
To be happy for my friends and family
What I don't want to do in life is wish
To wish for something is like a hit and miss
You may get what you want, you may get
nothing at all
The world seems so big, makes you seem so
small
It makes you think about the big questions
What if we weren't even here,
What if no one noticed if I disappeared

Too many what ifs to think about "why" and
"how"
It's better to live life to the fullest in the here and
now

What memories?

My head is numb
My mind feels empty
I don't know how I feel about all these missing
memoires
The time had come for them to go
Do I really need them? No, no I don't.

Your name is gone
Your name is erased
I can't bring it back not even your face
I can't look forward, I can't look back
All this emptiness, makes me want to have a
panic attack
There's nothing up there, my minds a blank slate
I don't know if I'll ever feel again, not at this rate

Do I regret it? Yes, kinda, no
I thought it'd help me move on and let go
But now I feel like a part of me is lost
It was probably for the better, but at what cost?
If I think about it too long, my head starts to hurt
I thought this was a good idea, now I'm not sure
I can't go back I've sealed my fate
I can't turn back time, I guess it too late

I won't let them go
I won't let these tears fall
These tears that I have, shouldn't be for you at
all
This feeling of numbness will eventually be
gone
All of our conversations, are now a bittersweet
song
And what should I do when they all come back
I'll turn my head away and hope the world turns
to black
I think they are gone, I made them go away,
And as much as I want them back, I think it's
better this way

Words Sharper than Knives

Some words cut deeper than knives
I knew that it was over in a blink of an eye
I thought I could save us, I thought I could try
But I knew it was hopeless, I didn't even cry
The words that hurt most are the ones that are
unsaid
I should've spoken up, but I shut my mouth
instead
I'm sorry I don't know how to communicate
I know I'm not perfect, I know I'm not a saint
Opening up gets harder each time
When I try speak up, it feels like a crime
People don't listen, people don't care
All my words disperse into empty thin air
So now I won't open up, I won't talk to you
Cause all past conversations are meaningless
and never follow through
But the words that hurt most that I can't seem to
forget
What you said to me, I knew it over, everything
went south
"Because honestly, I've been thinking about you,
and everytime I do, I question myself."

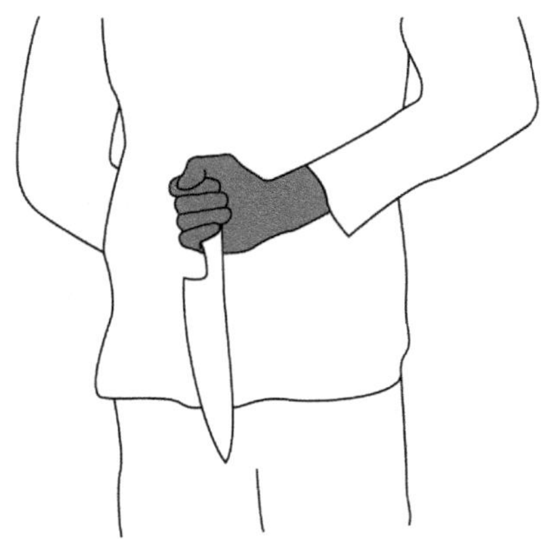

Saying sorry doesn't mean anything if you keep doing it

Why do I have to keep telling you the same
thing
I hate repeating myself
I wish that you could just listen to me
I hate repeating myself
I don't like having to tell you over and over that
things need to change
I hate repeating myself
I want us to work out, so we can be happy
It seems like you don't want to do this, not even
for me
Maybe if I tried a little harder
Spoken a little softer
Supported you a little more often
We could have made it out
Out of the pit we were spirling in
But I guess saying sorry doesn't mean anything
It doesn't mean anything when you're the one
who quit
I don't blame you, I would've too
But maybe we could have sat down and talked it
through
All the unsaid things that should've been said
Are now a bunched up mess inside my head

But are we going to continue this forth and back
I tell you this and you tell me that
nothings going to change if we don't fix our shit
Because saying sorry doesn't mean anything if
you keep doing it

A First for Everything

Everyone has a first for everything
There are the happy times that make good
memories
There are the hard times that make us stronger
For the next you go through it, you'll stand up
longer
The first time you held a baby in your arms
The first time you cried your eyes out because of
a love you lost
The first time you locked eyes with that person
you liked
The first time you reached the top of the
mountain you hiked
The first time you felt so numb all you could do
was stare into oblivion
The first time you healed yourself so you could
love again
The first time you and your best friend laughed
so hard you cried
The first time you stared at the love of your life
and sighed
You sighed because you gave a second chance
and found better
You found better because you're not a quitter

The first time you sat and stared at the world in
awe
In love with the things that God has done
The sad time you had to say goodbye to your
mom
The moment you realized she will be forever
gone
The first time you finally asked for help
Because you knew you couldn't do it by yourself
The first time you bought and drove your first
car
The first time you got the perfect job
The first time bought you first place the moment
you realized you were saved by God's grace
These are the moments, the firsts, that make us
unique
These are the moments that make you, you.

The Letter never Delivered

Up all night, I'm staying up late
I don't think I'll get to sleep at this rate
I'm hurting right now, I don't know what to do
I look at clock, its 11:52
I grab my phone and find things I don't like
I turn it off, shut my eyes, the tears are flowing, I
start to cry
I guess three months is enough time to think
To think, to consider, make your thoughts come
to sync
I hope it works out for the better
All the words I never said are in this letter
I write and I type faster than lightning
My thoughts, my fingers, different speeds its
frightening
I stop, I pause, to think, to look back
I turn off my phone, the room goes black
A frustrated sigh, I need to forget
But I need to finish this, my heart is set
Set to forget the memories that haunt me
I look at the time again, 12:33
I type and write I scribble and scramble
I hope this makes sense, cause all I did was
ramble

10 samsung note pages later, I'm finished, I'm
done
This is the letter, this is the one
The one that has all my feelings and thoughts
explained
Do I feel better or are my feelings still
unchanged
Maybe, maybe they are
My heart is slowing healing, yet there is still a
scar
The time says 1:20 in the morning
The memories don't feel as haunting
I smile to myself, the room is cold, I give a little
shiver
This letter for you, will never be delivered

What it feels like to have a broken heart

I want to try again
Because I'm feeling so lonely
Crying in the shower doesn't do anything for me
To give someone a chance is to give them my
heart
But how do I give something, when its in a
million parts
Picking up the pieces one by one
Gets harder each day when every piece I get
stung
A misunderstanding there, and a lie here
I can't do anything because I messed it up
I'm standing off the deep end, not knowing
where to jump
Am I capable to love again, or will it go
downhill
When I think of what I did, it makes my heart
stand still
And not in a good way, because what I did was
wrong
I made you feel like you couldn't get to know me
at all
My heart aches and breaks every time I think of
that day

But I just sat there and stared and let you have it
your way
I hope that you're well, no really I do
Don't worry about me, one day I'll pull through
You deserve the world and all the stars
I'll just keep my broken heart and my scars

My only friend is darkness

My only friend is darkness
I try to escape, but I'm on a harness
He says he likes my company
I sigh turn away very sullenly
Talking and games he tries to converse
I shake my head, I'm in my own universe
I don't want to speak I don't want to talk
I just want to remember all the things that I've
lost
At night darkness whispers secrets in my ears
Secrets of nightmares, tears and of fears
I try to turn away but he's in my head
Telling me things that shouldn't have been said
The dark is so bright I close my eyes
I try to escape but I can't, so I cry